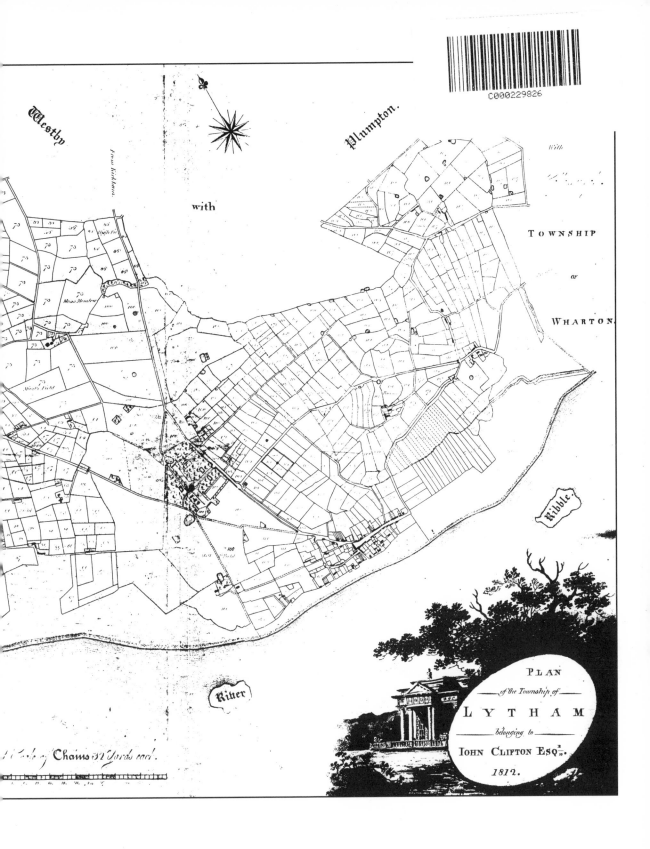

Westby

Plumpton.

with

with

TOWNSHIP

OF

WHARTON.

Moss Meadow

Ribble

River

PLAN
of the Township of
LYTHAM
belonging to
JOHN CLIFTON ESQ^R.
1812.

LYTHAM ST ANNE'S
A Pictorial History

Lytham from the pier, *c*.1900. 'Lytham has improved vastly. From a waste of blowing sand, unprotected beach, and a not overclean, straggling village, it has, within a man's lifetime, become one of the pleasantest, cleanest and well-built little towns in all England', *Lytham Times*, 29 November 1882.

LYTHAM ST ANNE'S
A Pictorial History

To Eddie Brown, best wishes from the author R.A. Haley

R.A. Haley

Phillimore

1995

Published by
PHILLIMORE & CO. LTD.,
Shopwyke Manor Barn, Chichester, West Sussex

ISBN 0 85033 986 3

Printed and bound in Great Britain by
BIDDLES LTD.
Guildford, Surrey

List of Illustrations

Frontispiece: Lytham from the pier, *c.*1900

Acknowledgements

I would like to thank the following people for their help in the compilation of this book: Ted and Ann Lightbown, my mother and father, W. John Smith, F.S.A., James Hilton (Lord of the Manor of Lytham), Graham D. Boyes, The Collodion Collection of Lytham, Norma and Keith Darley, David Moore, Richard Hindle, James Lee, Peter Stebbings, Cyril Defriez, Kath, Philip and Ian at St Anne's and Ansdell Libraries, Lancashire Records Office, Preston and the staff at the Lytham St Anne's Express Office in Wood Street.

This book is dedicated to the various local historians who, over the years, have assisted me in my research but have since passed away. These are the late: Kathleen Eyre, John Kennedy, Barry Dawson, Frank Dean and Walter Brayshaw.

I am indebted to the following people and organisations for allowing me to reproduce documents and photographs which they own: J.C Hilton esq., Lord of the Manor of Lytham, 2, 4; The Collodion Collection, Lytham, 3, 19, 21, 23, 28, 42, 45, 52, 63, 99; St Anne's Library, 7, 18, 38, 47, 76, 94; W. John Smith, F.S.A., 8, 16, 26, 34, 37, 39, 51, 54, 59, 62, 64-9, 74, 75, 77, 84-8, 90-3; Ted Lightbown, 24, 58; Peter Stebbings, 31, 107; Richard Hindle, 73; Ian McLoughlin, 155; John Salisbury, 32, 33; the late Barry Dawson, 72, 80, 89, 104, 109, 119, 120, 123, 130, 162, 163, 166-71, 174, 175; the late Frank Dean, 20, 150, 173, 176; the late Walter Brayshaw, 11, 46, 55, 56, 146, 149, 160, 169.

Introduction

This text spans over a thousand years of history to look at the various factors that influenced the development and character of modern Lytham St Anne's. The illustrations should help the reader to follow this development in which thousands of acres of field, common and sand dune gave way to streets, houses and hotels.

Modern Lytham St Anne's lies to the south west of the Fylde, alongside the Ribble, the Ribble estuary and Irish Sea, and bears little relation to the bleak, ill-drained expanse that existed there before the Norman Conquest. Most of the land was bog, marsh and moss and there was at least one mere. The hillocks and rising ground such as Ballam, Saltcotes and Mythop were possibly sites of early settlement. Here, the earliest farmers would begin to tackle the problem of draining the land which was in constant danger of inundation from the sea, river and mere.

Legend asserts that a Celtic church or oratory existed here along the coast at a place known as Kilgrimol. Evidence for its existence can be found in a charter of 1190-9 which mentions the burial yard of Kilgrimol (but not the church) as being near the boundary of Lytham and Layton (modern Blackpool).

Another legend is that the remains of St Cuthbert, removed by the monks from Lindisfarne during the Danish raids, were brought ashore at Lytham *c.*882 on their journey to Chester-le-Street and final resting place at Durham. A modern roadside cross in Church Road, Lytham, erected on a much older base, is said to mark the place where the sarcophagus rested.

After the Norman Conquest, Lytham was a small portion of the lands given by King John to Roger de Poitou. At the time of the Domesday Survey 'Lidun' contained two caracutes of land; there is no mention of a church.

Some one hundred years later Lytham was held by Roger Fitz Roger who in 1190-99 granted all his land at 'Lethum', along with the church, to the monks of Durham 'for the establishment there of a house of their order'. The Foundation Charter of Lytham Priory still exists and gives the boundaries of the Manor of Lytham with many place names still recognisable:

> ... from the ditch on the western side of the burial yard of Kilgrimol [site of St Anne's or Ansdell] above which I have erected a cross ... over towards the east alongside the Cursidmere [on Lytham Moss], over the great moss and the stream unto Balholm [Ballam], in a straight line over the moss ... unto the northern side of the Estholmker [Eastham], following eastward unto the margin of water [Wrea Brook] which comes from Bircholm [Wrea Green] and separates Eastholmker and Briningker [Bryning] ... southward unto the ford between Estholm and Couburgh, thence returning toward the west, and ... southward over the moss into the pull [Lytham Pool] beyond Snarlsalte [Saltcotes] where it falls upon the sea shore.

The church mentioned in this charter is thought to be the one built at about the time of the Norman Conquest to replace a ruinous one (possibly at Kilgrimol).

The boundaries given are almost exactly the same as those of the Borough of Lytham St Anne's which existed until 1974.

The monks of Durham subsequently established a Benedictine Priory at Lytham which existed for over 300 years. The site of the original priory is thought to have been near St Cuthbert's Church, but at the time of the Dissolution it stood on the site of Lytham Hall. The priory derived an income from the rents and tithes of Lytham. They improved the land by draining and enclosing it and by the mid-1300s there were three mills in Lytham operated by horse, wind and water power. Horses, cattle, sheep, pigs and poultry were bred on their estate and the River Ribble and Irish Sea provided fish.

In 1539 the Prior of Durham leased the Manor of Lytham to Thomas Dannet for 80 years at an annual rent of £48 19s. 6d. However, the Dissolution of the Monasteries resulted in the ownership of Lytham passing to the Crown and in 1549 Thomas Dannet applied to the Crown for a reduction in rent. The King's surveyor reported that:

> the capital house and manor of Lethum and the houses and buildings belonging to the same stand in great danger by reason of the rage of sand there and must shortly be taken down and builden in some other place.

Hundreds of acres of common pasture, arable land, marsh and four cottages with gardens had been lost by blowing sand. The rent paid to the Crown was subsequently halved.

Over the centuries that followed sand covered most of the land along the coast, forming a sand dune belt from Blackpool to Lytham which stretched inland, in some parts beyond the present railway.

The manor of Lytham had several owners and tenants until 1606 when it was acquired by Cuthbert Clifton of Westby. The Clifton family held Lytham for over 350 years; they owned every inch of land as well as all cottages and farms upon it. All the inhabitants of Lytham were tenants, leasing buildings and land on short-term feudal leases. This allowed the Cliftons to develop their estate as they wished and gave them great power and influence over their tenants.

After the purchase of Lytham, Cuthbert Clifton had a hall built incorporating parts of the old priory buildings. He also set about improving his estate by enclosing the Hawes (site of Ansdell and St Anne's) by an Act of 1616, and draining this in turn led to more farms and cottages and a greater income from rents. With the exception of the Civil War period when the Catholic Cliftons fought on the Royalist side, resulting in the confiscation of their estates, they made steady progress in agricultural improvements.

The vulnerability of their estate was demonstrated by an inundation of the sea on 18-19 December 1719 when sea defences, ditches and the winter crop of corn were destroyed. Forty dwellings along with barns, hay, household goods and cattle were all washed away. Some good did come out of this disaster. The money raised by charity for the homeless tenants could not be divided due to disagreements. It was put in trust to educate poor children, a school was erected at Lytham and the remainder invested in agricultural land at Layton. By sheer good fortune much of the charity's land at Layton was, a century later, in the centre of the rapidly expanding resort of Blackpool. Rents from this land built Heyhouses, King Edward VII and Queen Mary Schools.

In the 1750s the architect John Carr of York was commissioned to erect the present Georgian Lytham Hall. This incorporated parts of the Jacobean Hall and was completed in 1764. Agricultural improvements by the Cliftons were aided by Lytham Agricultural Society, formed about 1836. At this time 'the whole country was undrained, totally unsuitable for grazing sheep and but little more suited to the keeping of cattle or the growth of vegetables'. Ditches, dykes, *kops* and watercourses were constructed. Parts of the estate resembled a Dutch landscape.

In the period *c.*1840-80 improvements were made to the farms and labourers' cottages on the Cliftons' estate, many of which were run-down hovels. Slate replaced thatch, new windows were pierced and dripstones added as well as bargeboards and porches, chimneys and finials, thus giving an overall Gothic appearance. In most cases the original fabric was retained and added to, others were totally rebuilt, some were left untouched.

Industry in Lytham

The industrial revolution which transformed many northern towns into manufacturing districts on the whole bypassed the Fylde coast. Lytham in the mid-1800s was described as a place 'destitute of commerce and manufacture ... almost entirely destitute of minerals and antiquities ... totally destitute'.

This statement was not entirely true. Hand-loom weaving had gone on in most of the cottages on the estate; there might be two or three looms in each cottage and women worked by candlelight in the long winter evenings. Their work was taken to Preston on the backs of donkeys by a carrier who also brought back their provisions and materials. This cottage industry had all but died out in the area by the 1840s.

Boat-building had gone on at Lytham in a small way for many years and as the Ribble was, for larger vessels, unnavigable, they discharged their cargoes at either Lytham or Freckleton which were then taken up the river on lighters to Preston. A dock was built in the early 1840s and in 1888 Richard Smith moved his shipbuilding and engineering company to Lytham Creek.

In the early 1850s Thomas Clifton had an 'extensive tile manufactory' at Lytham 'under the management of Mr. Alexander Faulkener', but this appears to have been a short-lived venture. The vast majority of the population were employed in the age-old pursuits of farming, fishing, shrimping and collecting shellfish.

The industrial revolution which transformed the northern towns also transformed Lytham, not into a manufacturing district but into a resort.

Lytham as a resort

By the late 1700s Lytham had started to attract visitors from inland. Sea-bathing was in vogue and the spectacle of strangers in search of its health-giving properties immersing themselves in, and drinking of, the sea-water must have been a great source of amusement to the weather-hardened rustics whose families had fished and farmed the coast for generations. Visitors came in sufficient numbers to justify the erection of two hotels, the *Wheatsheaf* and the *Clifton Arms*, both in Clifton Street, in 1794.

Lytham, however, did not become a resort overnight. It was a gradual process, and the main concern of the Cliftons was agriculture. In *c.*1804 a windmill was erected on what is now Lytham Green but what was then known as 'the Marsh'. The Marsh may in times past have been a swamp but in 1804 it was a narrow tract of sandy waste and dunes that extended from the foot of the Starr Hills (large sandhills opposite Ansdell) to Stanner End in Lodge Pool, and from the shingle ridge (stanner) along the beach to the cottages in Clifton Street.

By 1813 two more hotels had opened as well as new shops and a house of confinement. Houses had also been erected facing the Marsh (now West, Central and East Beach), some private and others 'for the accommodation of strangers during visiting season'. Sea bathing was facilitated by three two-wheeled bathing machines and a bathhouse had been erected on the Marsh, on the site now occupied by the *Queen's Hotel*.

Lytham's other attractions at this time included two new bowling greens and annual races. Travelling minstrels also played here regularly.

Visitors could then walk through Lytham Hall Park where there were gardens, hothouses and greenhouses, shrubberies, woods and plantations. A popular spot here was 'the Mount' which was in fact an ice house constructed of brick and covered in earth from an adjacent site. The pit formed by the excavations was filled with water and stocked with fish and when it froze over the ice would be thrown in the ice house so as to preserve food. On top of 'the Mount' was an ornamental flagstaff and visitors could walk to the top to gain fine views of the Fylde, Westmorland, Cumberland and, in clear weather, the Cambrian mountains.

By 1830 much of the marsh had been levelled, chained off, and a public walk was formed alongside the beach. The *Wheatsheaf Hotel* had been demolished and in its place stood Dicconson Terrace and a billiard room. Coaches called at all hours from Preston and, during the season, from Blackburn, Halifax and various parts of Yorkshire.

Lytham was progressing as a resort, but it was a painfully slow process. The main reasons for this lay in the old feudal life-leases.

If an individual wished to erect any property in Lytham, he could only get a lease for 40 years. Once his property was erected he could not sell or let the building without the consent of the Cliftons or their agent. He also had to abide by other 'obsolete reservations and covenants' and when the lease expired the land and buildings upon it became the property of the Cliftons. Thus, there was little incentive to build.

By 1830 the terms of these leases had been extended to 60 years and about 1846 to 99 years; the 999-year leases came later.

Docks, Ship Canal and Railway Developments

All attempts to make the Ribble navigable to Preston having failed, in 1834 an equally unsuccessful scheme proposed the construction of a ship canal for vessels of up to 200 tons. In 1843 a dock was constructed at Lytham and leased to the Ribble Navigation Company until 1863. In July 1845 construction of the Lytham Branch line by the Preston & Wyre railway began, opening on 17 February 1846. The passenger terminus was on Station Road and a branch line ran to the new docks. The railway, docks and, soon after, extension of leases to 99 years brought about an era of prosperity.

Local Government in Lytham

A description of Lytham in the 1820s and 30s stated that:

it had the appearance of a village built anyhow showing no trace of design as to why or wherefore the houses had been pitched upon the particular sites where they stood. There was a road [Clifton Street] either side of which were cottages of mud and brick and cobble with small blear-eyed-looking windows, roofs of straw thatch, and with their back yards to the front ... where all animal and vegetable refuse ... was piled up, in slovenly fashion on the road near the main entrances to the houses. There was an open channel to take away household slops etc., a purpose it served efficiently when there was a heavy downfall of rain; at all other times it was merely a receptacle of filth which, festering there, gave an odour ...

Poor housing, inadequate sanitation and lack of basic amenities led, in 1847, to the Lytham Improvement Act, laying the foundations of local government. This Act vested the management of Lytham's local affairs in a board of commissioners who started to develop, amongst other things, a general system of sewerage, paving and roads. Within a year the Lytham Commissioners had erected the long-needed Market Hall and had the gasworks under construction. The streets were first lit by gas on 28 October 1850.

The Lytham Commissioners played an important rôle in the building up of Lytham which went on apace in the late 1800s, with the erection of churches, shops, houses, hotels and the laying out of Lytham Green to its present extent. From 1894-1921 their work was continued by Lytham Urban District Council.

Limited Companies

Before the 1860s most of Lytham's development had been carried out by the Clifton Estate and the Improvement Commissioners. This situation changed after limited liability legislation was passed in Parliament resulting in a flurry of new local companies in the early 1860s. The Lytham Baths & Assembly Room Company provided public and private baths and indoor entertainment. The Blackpool & Lytham Railway Company opened up Lytham common for development and provided a rail link between the two towns. The Fylde Water Works piped water which previously had to be drawn from wells or taken from ditches. The Pier Company provided a promenade and a jetty for boats and pleasure steamers. These early companies were not a great success. Within a few years the baths company was wound up and the baths maintained for many years by the Cliftons. The companies that were set up to run the pier collapsed at least twice before 1900. The railway was not profitable and was purchased by the L & Y and LNWR Companies in 1871. They already owned the Lytham Branch Line and joined the two railways, making a double track railway from Kirkham, along the coast to Blackpool, which was completed and opened on 1 July 1874. Despite their failure these companies provided much needed entertainment and encouraged the further development of the estate.

Lytham's rapid development of amenities for visitors during the period 1840-65 was followed by stagnation in the 1870s and '80s giving rise to the following comment in 1882:

Long ago, Lytham made a spurt, placed herself nearly abreast of her competitors and then stood still. So she has been standing ever since.

With the exception of Lowther Gardens (1878) and the pier pavilion (1892), there were no major additions to the resort's attractions and the town relied on the same old recipe to entice visitors. Instead, Lytham expanded as a residential town. Private residences in the form of lofty Gothic terraces were erected and continued to be erected until almost all the available plots in Lytham were built upon and the Cliftons' land agent looked west to the sand dunes for further sites.

Ansdell

In the early 1850s the Cliftons tried to push development of Lytham westwards, opening up the Starr Hills area. Hulking was constructed along part of the seafront just beyond St Cuthbert's Church, the sand and shingle above cleared and the site advertised as 'plots for marine villas'. The first house erected on these plots was 'Fairlawn' for Mr. Eden, a Manchester solicitor. Later came 'The Elms', 'Riversleigh' and 'The Willows'.

In 1860 the Liverpool-born artist Richard Ansdell had a summer residence, 'Starr Hills', erected, taking its name from the surrounding dunes which lay between the large new villas and Commonside Road. Ansdell was no stranger to Lytham; he exhibited paintings of 'Lytham Sandhills' and 'Lytham Common' in the early 1850s and chose the site of his house for its solitude. The solitude he sought was soon broken. On 4 September 1861, the first sod of the Lytham & Blackpool Railway was cut by Colonel Clifton. This single-line railway opened in 1863 and passed to the rear of Ansdell's house where there was a halt known as 'Ansdell's Gate' and a level crossing. With engines chugging back and forth and the prospect of the railway opening up the dunes for development he sold 'Starr Hills' in 1864. The district that subsequently sprang up here, and in the Commonside area, took his name.

In 1878, the Lytham Land & Building Company was formed and leased 60 acres of land bounded by Clifton Drive, Cambridge Road, and Ansdell Road. The first houses to be built by this company were those on Cambridge Road near the old Ansdell Station, but most were built in the 1890s.

The late 1890s saw the development, by various builders, of Old Commonside and the new Rossall Road. In 1903 Woodlands Road Bridge was erected and the new Ansdell Station built there. Ansdell, although a district or extension of Lytham, developed like a village with its own shopping centre, Institute and churches, and it has retained much of its Edwardian character.

The West End and the new town in the dunes

The site upon which St Anne's now stands was, prior to the 1870s, known as the 'West End' of Lytham Manor. The only building on the seaward side of the railway was one pair of cottages which housed a gamekeeper and lighthouse keeper, and, on top of a huge sand dune, the lighthouse itself. All the land from Lytham to Blackpool was one vast tract of mountainous sandhills, protected from the sea by a huge bank of shingle. Inland, beyond the railway, were fields, farms and cottages, scattered here and there as far as Heyhouses Lane.

In 1872 the Clifton estate embarked on an ambitious scheme to develop this area into a new resort. That year Clifton Drive, a road to run along the coast cutting through the dunes from Lytham to Blackpool, was begun. St Anne's Road was then constructed to run inland, joining the main Lytham to Blackpool road via Headroomgate. The same year Eleanor Cecily Clifton erected a church, dedicated to St Anne, to serve the West End inhabitants as well as future churchgoers in the new resort.

In 1874 the church was completed, roads were nearing completion, and the Clifton Estate were advertising building plots at 'St Anne's-on-the-Sea' in the regional press. That same year Elijah Hargreaves, a Rossendale man who had helped to float several cotton mill companies in that district, joined with a group of other Rossendale businessmen to form a company that would develop the new resort of St Anne's. On 14 October 1874 the St Anne's Land & Building Company (hereafter referred to as

L & B Co.) was registered with share capital of £50,000. The Clifton Estate initially leased them 82 acres, and eventually 600 acres of land in the centre of the new resort. The company not only paid over £3,000 per year in ground rents to the Cliftons but were obligated to spend £70,000 on developing the town within a few years. Several smaller companies were also formed to construct and run a hotel, gasworks, and gardens, as well as a brick and tile works.

Initially, work went well. The hotel, gasworks, railway station and promenade were all completed by the end of 1876. Houses, schools, shops and new roads were under construction. Unfortunately, the L & B Co. had been formed just as the country was sliding into a trade slump which, with its ups and downs, lasted for most of the last quarter of the 19th century. The slump badly affected the building trade as house prices were often less than the cost of their construction and the rental value of many properties had halved by 1883.

The result of this was stagnation. Apart from the construction of the pier, the town made little progress. Three of the four smaller companies were wound up and absorbed into the parent company, which itself would have undoubtedly collapsed had it not been for Mr. W.J. Porritt. He owned several mills, including Sunnybank Mill at Helmshore, and profits from these went into the construction of the properties along North Promenade and North Drive. He built these ahead of demand, right through the slump, the stone coming from his family's quarries at Hasseldon and Torside. These substantial houses are known locally as Porritt houses.

St Anne's was unkindly described by a visitor in 1890 as being 'a poky little village on a sand hill where retired captains of industry indulged in golf and spent the evening of their days in quiet solitude'. Things were soon to change. In the 1890s prosperity returned and a building boom commenced. In the ten years 1881-91 the population of St Anne's had increased by about 1,300; the following decade it rose by over 4,200. The L & B Co. was once again back on its feet and it settled down to leasing land and improving its pier. When the visitor of 1890 returned to St Anne's in 1916 he described it as 'a veritable garden by the sea'.

Local Government in St Anne's

In its earliest years, St Anne's came under the jurisdiction of the Lytham Commissioners, but in 1878 a Local Board of Health gave St Anne's its own local government. Housed in one room in Matlock House, South Drive, its main tasks were to keep down the rates, avoid loans, and to move blown sand from the roads. In 1892, the Board embarked on a main drainage scheme for St Anne's. Two years later St Anne's Urban District Council replaced the Board. This was a very progressive council and improvement schemes that it initiated were the taking over and laying out of South Promenade (1896), the erection of electricity works, abattoirs, fire station and refuse destructor (1897-1902), paddling pool (1912), Ashton Gardens, Promenade baths (1913-16) and the purchase of trams (1919).

Companies that helped St Anne's prosper were the Public Hall Co. (1898), Carltons Cosy Corner Ltd. (1904) and the Empire Cinema Co. (1912). At St Anne's, though, other factors influenced its evolution. Private schools, convalescent homes and golf clubs all played a prominent rôle in publicising the town, attracting visitors and potential residents.

Fairhaven

Before development, this district was a narrow range of sand-dunes between Lytham and St Anne's on the seaward-side of Clifton Drive, protected from the sea by a ridge of shingle known locally as a 'stanner'. A second crescent-shaped 'stanner' formed a natural harbour which could be accessed from Granny's Bay.

In 1892, Thomas Riley, a Fleetwood contractor, took a lease of 264 acres of land with the intention of turning it into a resort in its own right. Named Fairhaven, from St Paul's travels, it was a colossal undertaking. The natural harbour was enclosed and shingle banks were strengthened to form a lake. An estate railway was laid from the main line, running around the lake and the full length of the estate. Sand-moving machines were imported from America to level the dunes and fill the dells.

Unfortunately Thomas' eldest son James, who was supervising the preparation of the site, fell ill and died at Christmas 1893; his only other son, Charles, was just 14 at this time. Thomas found the task of developing the estate too daunting and he sold out to a group of men who formed the Fairhaven Estate Company (1895) Ltd. The company carried on his work, but a scheme to extend the marine lake round the coast to St Anne's was abandoned after the inundation of 1896.

Fairhaven developed quickest at the Lytham and St Anne's ends of the estate and the middle section was leased to the Fairhaven Golf Club. In 1907-8 King Edward VII School was erected on the estate. The Golf Club left in 1923 and Queen Mary School was erected in 1929-30. By the start of the Second World War the vast majority of the estate was built upon.

Lytham and St Anne's during the First World War

During the First World War Lytham and St Anne's were used to train the newly formed brigades of field artillery recruited in West Lancashire by Lord Derby. Between February and August 1915 over 1,000 troops were billeted at Lytham and over 3,000 at St Anne's. The billet allowance paid to householders and lodging-house keepers was 3s. 4½d. per man per day and St Anne's took £50,000 in billet payments alone.

Later in the war Pioneer Battalions were billeted at Lytham whilst St Anne's was used for convalescent officers and soldiers. There was a home for Belgian refugees on East Beach, Lytham, a convalescent hospital at Chaseside, St George's Square, St Anne's, and at Ansdell 'Starr Hills' was a V.A.D. Hospital. Over 700 wounded soldiers passed through this latter hospital and the sundial in Lowther Gardens is a token of gratitude given by the soldiers who were restored to health by the skilful nursing of the ladies of 'Starr Hills'.

Anyone with a workshop was called into service. Local joiners and cabinet-makers were employed in making packing boxes for shells. Several garages made and finished the shell cases and noses. There were large munition factories at Squires Gate and Lytham. The engineering shop of the tramways was also employed in war work and the company helped run a parcel delivery service by tram between Lytham, St Anne's, Blackpool and Fleetwood. In 1918 a flying boat factory was erected at Lytham's East End. Women played their part too by fund-raising, nursing, munitions work and entering employment to fill the places of men away at the front. Despite the restrictions of wartime, the St Anne's Council succeeded in completing the open-air baths on the beach, the laying out of Ashton Gardens and erection of Ashton Pavilion.

1922-1939

The Borough of Lytham St Anne's was formed on Charter Day, 1 May 1922, reuniting the two districts, which were separated in 1878, and with boundaries the same as those of the ancient Manor of Lytham.

Although well-matched in that they were two middle-class resorts, the two councils were very different—Lytham's was laid back and St Anne's progressive. This fact, combined with the problem of distributing the Borough budget fairly between the two ends of the Borough was to be a source of trouble throughout its life.

These were the days when everything in the town seemed to be owned and run by local government. The Borough Council was responsible for all the parks, two swimming baths, recreation grounds, Lowther Pavilion, Ashton Pavilion, Fairhaven Lake, trams, buses, electricity, gas, fire stations, abattoirs, roads, pavements, sewers, street lighting and, amongst other things, collection and destruction of refuse. No wonder that one resident, about to shovel up some fresh manure for his roses from underneath the Borough's horse-drawn dustcart, was told by the council employee, 'Ya can't 'ave that—it belongs t'corporation'.

The ever-increasing rôle of local government continued unabated through the inter-war years. New gasworks at Eastham (1924), bus service (1923), town hall, cemetery, and promenade road (1925), gardens at Fairhaven Lake (1926), reconstruction of Lytham Baths (1928), mussel tanks and paddling pool on Lytham Beach (1934) and Outer Promenade, St Anne's (1934-9). The Second World War meant that further schemes were shelved.

During the years of the Depression the Fylde coast was described as being 'strewn with the wreckage of the cotton slump'. Many residents and visitors derived their income directly or indirectly from the Lancashire cotton belt. Many lost fortunes overnight and left their large mansions here to face an uncertain future. The tourist and shop trade was badly affected and the council cut its spending to keep the rates low—even the mayoral banquet of 1931 was cancelled to save £100.

Non-municipal developments between the wars included the new railway station at St Anne's (1925) and the conversion of 'Westwood' to a Miners' Home (1928). Lytham lost its pier pavilion by fire in February 1928 but the baths there were rebuilt in the same year. Lytham Palace Cinema opened in 1930 and the new Cookson's Exhibition Bakery opened in 1938.

The last Squire of Lytham was Mr. H. de Vere Clifton. He frittered away every last vestige of his inheritance. Between 1935 and 1939 he sold the ground rents of Lytham St Anne's and in the 1950s many of the farms on his estate were sold to the tenants. In the 1960s Lytham Hall and Park were sold to Guardian Royal Assurance. The Cliftons' final links with Lytham were severed in 1978 when Mr. Clifton transferred the Lordship of the Manor of Lytham to Mr. James Hilton esq. of Lytham. Lytham owes a debt of gratitude to Mr. Hilton for, apart from preventing the title going abroad, he also saved many important manorial documents from being sold and lodged them at the Lancashire Records Office. Mr. H. de Vere Clifton died in November 1979.

In 1962 the St Anne's Land and Building Company was purchased by and became a subsidiary of London-based Amalgamated Investment Co. Ltd. (A.I.P Co.). The A.I.P. Co. collapsed in 1975 and the St Anne's Land and Building Company and pier was purchased by the Webb family. They also purchased the Fairhaven Estate Company.

Housing Development

Since the last war most remaining plots of land near the sea have been built upon. The spread of St Anne's towards Blackpool was halted by Blackpool Aerodrome and the nature reserve. Builders have pushed development inland into the rural areas of the Borough. Agricultual land, along with farms, cottages and lodges, previously inhabited by the Cliftons' tenants, have been swept away by the tide of building development.

Guardian Royal Assurance opened up part of Lytham Hall Park for development. In St Anne's the A.I.P. Co. allowed the demolition of several large old properties to make way for flats. Since 1945 well over 150 buildings, including hotels, houses, shops and farms, have been demolished in Lytham St Anne's.

Lytham St Anne's as a resort

In 1974 Lytham St Anne's became part of Fylde Borough which has had to consider the needs of the rural Fylde as well as those of the coast. This was at a time when most British seaside resorts were going into decline, partly due to the foreign package holiday. Lytham St Anne's decline was hastened by the fires which destroyed the Moorish Pavilion (1974) and Ashton Pavilion (1977). Fylde Borough Council, apart from maintaining existing attractions, has had indoor swimming baths erected at St Anne's (1986) and renovated Lytham windmill which is now open to visitors.

Private investment in the resort over the last decade has resulted in various improvements in attractions for visitors. The derelict pierhead at St Anne's was demolished at Easter 1984 and the landward end, which comprises an amusement arcade, shops and short promenade, was renovated and balconies added. The Plaza (Empire) Cinema was converted into a Casino and Bingo Club. A Toy and Teddy Bear museum has opened and the large 'Pleasure Island' complex built on the site of the open-air baths. Hotels have undergone massive improvements with extensions providing leisure and conference facilities.

Some 200 years after the first hotels opened here, Lytham St Anne's looks set to enter the next century continuing to attract visitor and resident alike.

1 Cross Slack Hamlet, viewed from the 16th hole of the Old Links, in 1948. Kilgrimol Church and burial yard existed over 1,000 years ago on this coast somewhere between modern Lytham and Blackpool. Its site lost for over 500 years, some believe it to be Cross Slack and others that it is nearer Ansdell.

2 A plan drawn up *c.*1531 for the Butlers of the manor of Layton (left) to settle the boundary with Lytham manor (right). Between the two is the pasture known as 'the Hawes', which lay between the shore and Heyhouses Lane. Inland, the shaded area is Marton and Lytham Moss; the latter contained the 'Cursed Mere'. (L.R.O. DDC1 685 by kind permission of Mr. J.C. Hilton.)

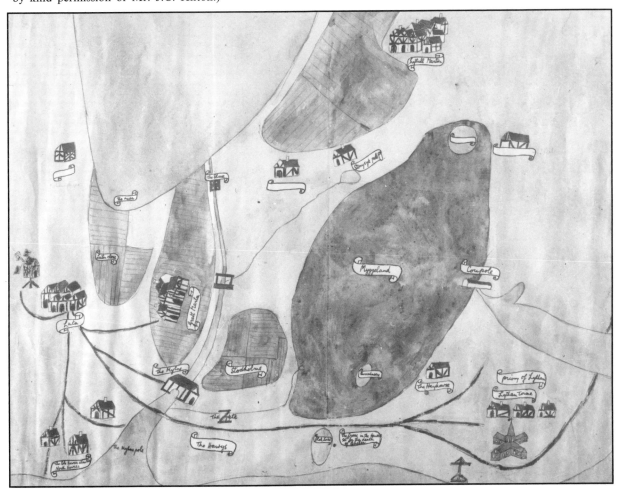

3 Shell Hill Cottages, Saltcotes, which stood on Saltcotes Road opposite the Roman Catholic Cemetery, were demolished c.1960. Situated on higher ground, it was possibly a site chosen by early settlers in the area. Originally one dwelling, this cottage was rebuilt in the 1700s. Salt panning went on in this district during the 16th century. Saltcotes Farm stood on Mythop Road.

4 Lytham, c.1610, after its acquisition by the Cliftons and the construction of the first Lytham Hall. Between the hall and St Cuthbert's Church is a peg and post windmill and the cottages represent the village of Lytham. (L.R.O. DDC1 1056 by kind permission of Mr. J.C. Hilton.)

5 Heyhouses Lane, c.1902, looking towards Lytham from near the present Premium Bonds site. The brick set in the cottage wall reads 'KOPS ALE'. This was the main road between Layton (Blackpool) and Lytham. Inland were the mosses of Marton and Lytham and, seawards, agricultural land and Lytham Common, enclosed under the Act of 1616.

6 Thatched cottages on Commonside (Ansdell) which were over 300 years old when they were demolished *c.*1950. Lytham Common stretched from here, around the coast to Cross Slack (Old Links) and lay between Commonside Lane (Church Road, St Anne's) and the coast. Blowing sand and sand dunes encroached on much of the land rendering it useless.

7 Looking west from the ditches and cops on agricultural land between Heyhouses Lane and Common Side Lane (Church Road, St Anne's), the latter being in the distance. To the left a stack of peat turfs is drying. Peat was used as a fuel and in some parts of the mosses so much was extracted that it lowered the height of the ground by several feet.

8 Designed by John Carr of York, Lytham Hall was completed in 1764 and is the finest Georgian mansion in Lancashire. The buildings to the rear are part of the old Jacobean Hall, converted into a courtyard. Panelling from the old hall was also incorporated.

9 Cottages in Regent Avenue, Heyhouses, *c.*1905. Although composed mainly of brick, parts of the foundations were constructed using pebbles. The date '1767' painted above an internal door probably indicated the year that they were rebuilt. In more recent years the Cross family lived in the left-hand cottage. In 1993 the whole row was taken down and rebuilt.

10 A farmer standing at the gate post of Boardman's Farm (erected 1767) in Regent Avenue. People born on this coast were termed 'sand grown'. In the 1820s local inhabitants were described as 'quite in keeping with the village, more picturesque than neat, sturdy and weather-defying enough but with no overweening desire to utilise the virtues of water, salt or otherwise upon themselves or their dwellings'.

"FINE DAY."
HEYHOUSES, LYTHAM.

B.A.
(COPYRIGHT.)

11 The *Clifton Arms Hotel* was erected in Clifton Street *c.*1794 and stood where Park Street is now. The *Wheatsheaf Hotel* was erected almost simultaneously on a site opposite, now occupied by Dicconson Terrace and the post office buildings. The *Ship Inn* was built *c.*1820.

12 In the 17th and 18th centuries there had been at least one peg and post windmill situated between Lytham Hall and St Cuthbert's Church. During the Napoleonic wars foreign imports of grain were cut off, resulting in the need for greater home production. The present windmill was erected yards from the sea on 'the Marsh', now Lytham Green, *c.*1804.

13 Blackpool Road, Ansdell, *c.*1912, looking towards the skew bridge from today's entrance to Forest Drive. The old Blackpool to Lytham Road passed through the old gates at Regent Avenue, into Lytham Hall Park, past the hall, entering Lytham at Market Square. Increasing traffic resulted in the construction of the present road and pebble wall skirting the estate *c.*1830.

14 James Fair, agent to the Cliftons' estates from 1836. He was very progressive; £250,000 was spent erecting farmhouses, cottages, making roads, laying drains and watercourses. He was responsible for the well-planned layout of Lytham's streets and its improvement as a resort. His son, Thomas was agent from 1862 to 1910.

15 St Cuthbert's Church, 1835. The increasing population of Lytham, combined with visitors during the season, filled the parish church to capacity and in 1834 the present church was erected in Tudor style. Church House (left), a dower house for the Cliftons, was rebuilt in Gothic style and later became the vicarage.

16 Roman Catholic Mass was held at Lytham Hall until 1800 when a tithe barn just outside Lytham Hall Park was 'fitted up as a chapel', described in 1830 as 'a plain white oblong building lighted by Norman windows from an eastern basement'. At this time the priest lived at 'The Woodlands'. In 1839 St Peter's Church was erected in Clifton Street; the tower was added in 1878.

17 Greaves farm, Headroomgate, *c.*1910. An example of a farm given Gothic treatment with steeply pitched roof, finials and bargeboards. This farm was for many years occupied by the Greaves family and still stands on Headroomgate Road, St Anne's.

18 These cottages in Clifton Street are typical examples of Estate cottages that underwent improvement during the 19th century. The thatch has given way to slate and is surmounted by finials; enlarged windows have dripstone mouldings above. These cottages were demolished in 1895 to make way for extensions to Lytham Institute and the erection of shops.

19 Church Farm, Commonside, renovated during the mid-1800s, and seen here in the 1890s, shortly before the surrounding fields were built upon. Its name suggests that it may have some connection with the Roman Catholic Chapel (1800-39); the priest lived nearby at 'The Woodlands'. This part of the Commonside has become part of Ansdell.

20 The classical façade of Lytham's first railway station in Station Road, c.1950. Opened in 1846, inside was an octagonal booking office with domed roof. The platforms were covered by an arched roof, supported by 12 wooden arches bolted together. In 1874 this station was closed to passengers and used as a goods station. It was demolished in the 1960s to make way for the fire station.

21 Seafield School, Seafield Road, founded in 1847 by the Misses Tait and later run by Mr. John Sisson Slater. It was a boarding and day school accommodating about 50 boys. The playing fields in front were also used by Pembroke House School from the 1890s and were cut through by the road linking Lytham Promenade with Clifton Drive, c.1931. The school closed in 1937.

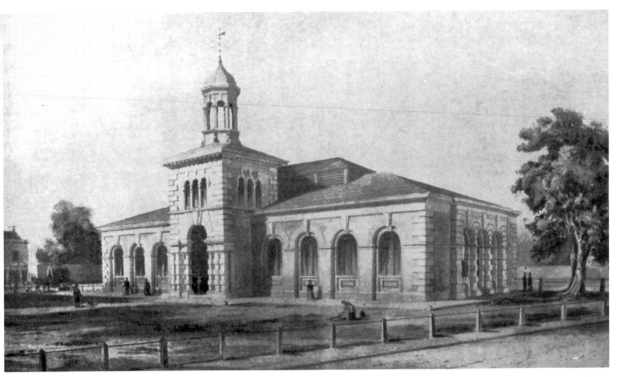

22 The Market Hall as originally constructed. Built at a cost of over £1,000 by the newly formed Lytham Commissioners whose office was in the tower, it was classical in design and enclosed by elm trees. The tower was raised in 1872 to receive a clock, the gift of Lady Eleanor Cecily Clifton. Lack of trade resulted in its conversion to shops in the 1890s.

23 Because the boundary of the Manor of Lytham extended to the centre of the River Ribble, the rights of anchorage and wreck, normally held by the Crown, were held by the Cliftons. The Custom House seen here was erected on Lytham Green, c.1850, replacing an office in Bath Street. Customs were taken anchored from vessels on the beach and in Lytham Pool.

24 West Beach, Lytham in the 1850s, by which time most of the seafront was built up and most of Lytham Green laid out. The resort was advancing in the post-railway era of prosperity with longer leases for land, supply of gas, and making of roads, pavements and sewers.

25 Pebbles had been used for centuries in the construction of buildings, yards, roads and walls. From the 1830s they were used as a decorative feature in pavements, such as those in Bath Street, and in buildings, such as the lifeboat house, custom house and hospital. Examples at St Anne's are the garden walls, North Promenade and the ornamental bridge on South Promenade.

26 The Bath House on East Beach was, in the early 1850s, managed by a Mrs. Middlehurst. In 1857 this building was demolished and the *Neptune Hotel* erected on the site. It was later renamed the *Queen's Hotel*. The two Georgian houses to the left were erected *c.*1828.

27 Starr Hills, built amongst the dunes as a summer residence for Richard Ansdell R.A. in 1860. During the First World War it was a hospital for wounded soldiers and in the Second World War it was a Distribution Centre. It is now a Methodist Convalescent Home.

28 The Georgian-style Clifton Estate Offices in Hastings Place, *c*.1890, were erected on or near the old road to Lytham Hall which was cut off by the new railway in the early 1860s. In this building the future development of Lytham was planned and the Clifton tenants paid their rents.

29 In 1861 construction of the Blackpool to Lytham railway started. About this time the old *Clifton Arms Hotel* in Clifton Street was demolished so that Park Street could be cut through and Ballam Road constructed to Higher Ballam. A new road to Lytham Hall was made, entered by these gates, standing just off Ballam Road.

30 The £60,000 Blackpool to Lytham Railway scheme was completed in 1862 and opened on 4 April 1863. A terminus was constructed at Ballam New Road. This railway had no connection with the Preston & Wyre Railway which had its terminus in Station Road. In 1872-4, when the two railways were joined, the Blackpool and Lytham terminus was rebuilt as a through station and is pictured here *c.*1900.

31 Ansdell's Gate, a halt on the Lytham-Blackpool railway to the rear of Richard Ansdell's house. There was a level crossing and a Gothic-style booking office where passengers obtained a small flag to wave the train to a halt. Ansdell Station was built here, with a footbridge in 1901. In 1903 the present station was erected at Woodlands Road.

32 Lytham Baths and Assembly Rooms, *c.*1867. Erected by a private company at a cost of £6,700, they were opened on 4 April 1863. Water for the baths was pumped from the sea by a 'powerful steam engine' and filtered. There were small individual baths as well as general swimming baths for both sexes, dressing, retiring, news and reading rooms as well as a room for concerts and balls capable of holding 350 people.

33 The *Clifton Arms Hotel* from the pier. The original two-storey building erected in 1840 is seen here, *c.*1867. The hotel was purchased by Mr. John Knowles who erected the three-storey extension to the right. The rest of the hotel was later raised to this height and sold to a private company about 1875.

34 The Foundation Stone of Lytham Congregational church was laid by Sir James Watts of Manchester on 17 October 1861; the church was completed in 1863. Built in the ornamental Gothic style, its tower and spire is 87 ft. in height, viewed here from Westby Street, and looking along Bannister Street, before the Police Station was built. The cottages are where Taverner's shop now stands.

35 A lifeboat had been stationed at Lytham since 1851; the lifeboat house which had housed the 'Clifton' and 'Eleanor Cecily' was to the east of the windmill. In 1863 the building pictured was erected to accommodate the 'Wakefield'. Sheltered seating was added *c*.1890 and the building is now a museum. The present lifeboat house opened in 1960.

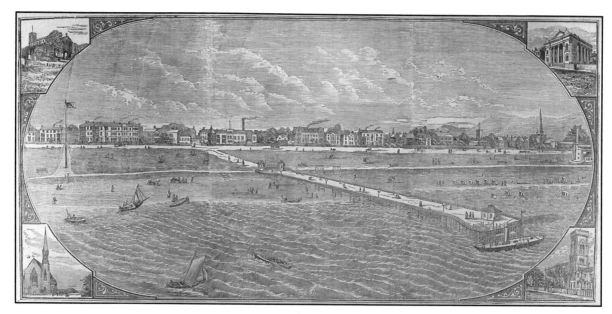

36 Lytham Pier, 1880. Designed by Eugenius Birch, it was 914 ft. in length with continuous seating and gas lamps along the deck. At the pier-head pleasure steamers docked and there was a lounging and waiting room. Excursion trains brought throngs of people for the ceremonial opening by Lady Eleanor Cecily Clifton on 17 April 1865.

37 The first service at Park Street Methodist Church, seen here *c.*1897, was on 23 September 1868. The previous chapel in Bath Street (1846) had become too small. Classical in style, the new church was faced with Longridge Stone and white brick. Stone columns and pilasters nearly 30 ft. high were surmounted by Corinthian caps, cornice, parapet and pediment. It seated about 500 persons.

38 After the collapse of its predecessor, this wooden lighthouse was erected by the Ribble Navigation Company in 1864 in splendid isolation on a large sand dune at the West End of Lytham. It ceased operation in 1890 and by the time it was demolished in 1901 streets and houses were encroaching upon it. Lightburne Avenue took its name from it.

39 Lytham Cottage Hospital opened on 3 August 1871 at the East End. John Talbot Clifton built and furnished it at a cost of £1,300 for the 'relief of the poor labouring under disease or accidents'. The running of the hospital was funded by voluntary contributions and the garden fêtes held on the three-acre grounds, until the N.H.S. was formed.

40 Hungry Moor was a 'frowsy and damp undrained piece of land fenced round and in its midst ... stood the ugliest of ugly wooden pumps'. In the 1870s this poor grazing land was laid out as Lowther Gardens at the expense of Col. Clifton. These were given to the town in 1905 and Lowther Pavilion was added by Lytham U.D.C. in 1921.

41 The *Talbot Hotel* was erected sometime between 1850 and 1872. In September 1873 the appropriately named Charles Brewster took over the licence from Alexander Seed. In the early 1900s when this photograph was taken Cornelius Salthouse was landlord and the order office was at the Bath Street entrance.

42 The Heyhouses Chapel of Ease, *c.*1885, dedicated to St Anne. The site chosen for this chapel was a field farmed by the Whiteside family. When Mr. Whiteside found out that there would be a burial ground he said that the land was not fit and that they would be all 'scrat up by the rabbits'. The chapel was completed in 1873. The new town took its name from the church and it became a separate parish in 1877.

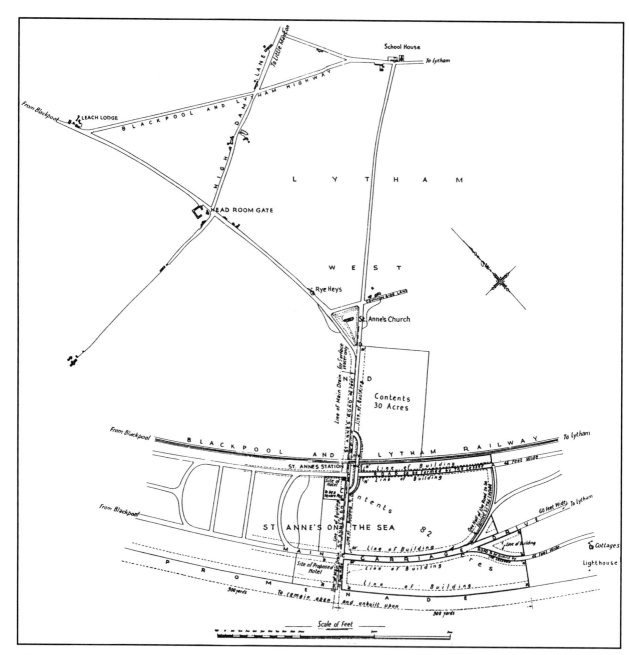

43 St Anne's, showing the initial 82 acres of sand-dunes leased by the Land and Building Company in December 1874. Clifton Drive South and St Anne's Road were under construction and joined the main Blackpool to Lytham road via Headroomgate. Note also Common Side Lane (Church Road), Old Heyhouses School, High Dam Lane (Kilnhouse Lane) and below Headroomgate is Twiggy Hill Lane (Highbury Road) which led to Gillett's (Cross Slack) Farm.

44 Alpha House, St Andrew's Road South was the first permanent building to be erected in St Anne's by the Land & Building Company; it was also the town's first post office, the first postmaster being Clement Rawstron. The building was converted into shops in 1907. In 1990, during renovations, a sandstone lintel was uncovered with the inscription 'Alpha House'; this was incorporated in the new shop front.

45 The foundation stone of St Anne's was laid in the foundations of the *St Anne's Hotel* by seven-year-old John Talbot Clifton at a ceremony on 31 March 1875. The hotel opened in April 1876; later a bowling green was added. The hotel was demolished in 1985. The *St Anne's Tavern*, shops and a car park now stand on the site.

46 The platform of St Anne's first railway station comprised 'four barrels and two planks' and 'the stationmaster's office, booking office and the whole box of tricks was contained in a green hut six ft. by four'. By December 1876 the railway company had completed the station pictured which, with extensions, served the town inadequately until 1925.

47 Lytham Institute, a working-men's reading room, was opened in the old Bath Street Methodist Chapel in the early 1870s. Its success resulted in the erection of this Gothic building, containing reading room, library, classrooms and billiards room, which opened in September 1878. The building was extended in 1896 and was given to the town in 1917.

48 Pembroke House School, seen here in 1905, was opened by Mr. E.R. Lightwood in these premises on Ansdell Promenade *c.*1878. The school was rather exclusive, fees were upwards of 80 guineas per annum and boys were prepared for university and commercial life. In the First World War it housed wounded soldiers and since 1934 the building has been the Stella Matutina Convent.

49 Sandy Knoll School for Boys, North Promenade, St Anne's, *c.*1911. This was the first building erected by W.J. Porritt. Opened in 1878, the school was run by the Thompson family (father, son and daughter). By the 1920s the school had moved into premises on Mayfield Road previously used as the Old Links Clubhouse (now the British Legion). The Porritt house which stood next to the *Majestic Hotel* was demolished in *c.*1960.

50 St Anne's Lifeboat House was erected next to the Methodist Chapel, Eastbank Road in 1880 and the first lifeboat, the *Laura Janet*, arrived the following year. It was this lifeboat that went down with all hands in the attempt to rescue the German barque *Mexico* in December 1886. All but two of the 16 crew in the Southport lifeboat also perished.

51 St Anne's Pier, designed by A. Dowson, C.E. of London, was constructed 1879-85 though open to the public by 1882. Graceful cast-iron arches supported the deck, 315 yards in length. At the entrance was the piermaster's office and at the pierhead a band kiosk and shelter. An iron extension stretched a further 40 yards out to the wooden jetty.

52 When St Anne's Pier was constructed, the jetty, pictured here *c.*1890, stood over 30 ft. in height and the North Channel which passed in front made it accessible at all states of the tide to pleasure steamers and yachts. Unfortunately the new channel from Preston out to sea caused the old North Channel to silt up. The last steamer called at the pier about 1910.

53 The jetty, St Anne's Pier, 1991. The loss of the North Channel robbed St Anne's of the scour of the tide, resulting in a build-up of sand. Since 1910 the level of the beach has steadily risen and the beach, which once sloped down to the jetty, is almost level. The sand has raised the height of the beach at the jetty by over 20 ft.

54 Lytham & St Anne's Golf Club was formed in 1886. Their headquarters were a room in the *St Anne's Hotel*. Their original links were bounded by the railway, St Anne's Road East, and Headroomgate. This photo was taken near present-day St Leonard's Road looking towards Blackpool, *c.*1896, and is now part of the Old Links Course.

55 A photograph by W. Kershaw, *c.*1886, looking from the site of the present St Anne's fire station inland, across the original links of Lytham and St Anne's Golf Club. In the distance are Morningside and Stanley Villas in St Anne's Road East. The train is on its way to Blackpool.

56 St Anne's Square, looking towards the sea *c*.1886, with Montauban School to the left, and the pier entrance in the centre. To the right are shops which today include the Midland Bank and William Hills. Shops on the other side of Garden Street (now the Woollen Mill and adjacent premises) were built by John Hindle of Accrington in 1877 and were the first shops in the Square.

57 In the last century ships were often seen anchored on Lytham beach between the windmill and the pier. All manner of cargoes were unloaded here including wheat and oats for the windmill, coal for the wealthier households and beer for the inns and hotels.

58 Festivities at Lytham to celebrate the golden jubilee of Queen Victoria in 1887 included a banquet, ball, bonfire, procession, regatta, sports and open-air fête in Lowther Gardens (pictured). When Lytham celebrated the golden jubilee of George III (1810) '300 children were regaled on cake and wine in Market Square'. In 1887, the influence of the temperance movement ensured that they had 'cakes and tea'.

59 St Anne's High School for Girls, North Promenade, built in 1887 for the Misses Sharpe and Hall. The school grounds backed onto Clifton Drive. Extremely successful, the school expanded into the adjoining house and in 1924 moved to its present site at Windermere. The building pictured became the *Princes Hotel* in 1939 and since 1984 has been owned by the Ormerod Trust. *Left.*

60 The worst disaster in the history of the lifeboat service occurred in December 1886 when 27 men aboard the St Anne's and Southport lifeboats all perished in an attempt to rescue the crew of the German barque *Mexico*. The monument to the 13 crew of the St Anne's lifeboat *Laura Janet* was unveiled on 23 May 1888. *Right.*

61 Lytham Creek, *left*, where Liggard Brook enters the Ribble. In 1888 Richard Smith moved his shipbuilding yard from Preston to this site. At this time the navigation of the Ribble was being improved by the construction of a new deep channel from Preston, out to sea. This caused the old North Channel that passed by Lytham and St Anne's to silt up.

62 The Abraham Ormerod Convalescent Home, *below left*, was erected on the beach beyond North Promenade, St Anne's, by the Misses Ormerod of The Elms, Lytham, in memory of their father, Mr. A. Ormerod of Todmorden. Opened in 1890, children from the polluted industrial towns were sent here to convalesce in the bracing sea air. In later years a home for the mentally handicapped, it was demolished in 1984.

63 St Anne's Roman Catholic Church, *below*, was erected at the foot of the Crescent in 1890. In 1925-7 the west front (pictured) was taken down and the church extended towards the road. The Roman Catholic School was erected in St Alban's Road in 1896; the present school in Kenilworth Road was built in 1968 and subsequently enlarged. The Catholic Social Centre opened in 1970.

64 Part of the Lytham and St Anne's Club's nine-hole ladies' course now occupied by Oxford Road and the Parish Rooms. In the centre is St Anne's Parish Church and to the left a house and cottage which stood next to Heyhouses School. The tower had been added to the church in 1890; the steeple was removed about 1898.

65 Clifton Drive South, viewed from a sand-dune (now Orchard and Bromley Roads) in 1896. On the left is Kilgrimol School for Boys, built for John Allen in 1875 and opened as the District Club in 1931. To the right is the lifeboat house in Eastbank Road and the Methodist Church, opened for worship in October 1892.

66 Lytham Pier, *right*, after the addition in 1892 of the £12,000 pavilion halfway along the deck. In 1895 the Pier Company, yet again, collapsed and another was formed. This company enlarged the pavilion in 1901 and converted the band enclosure at the pierhead into a floral hall. During a storm in 1903 two Ribble Navigation Company sand barges smashed the deck between the entrance and the pavilion.

67 Clifton Square, Lytham, *below*, looking inland, *c*.1893. The building on the left stood on the corner of Henry Street and was demolished in 1898. The old row of shops was built about 1830 and all except Edmundsons were demolished in 1898. Lytham Post Office is partially obscured by the trap driver.

68 Market Square, Lytham, *c*.1893, *below right*, showing the Market Hall after the erection of the clock (1872) and the drinking fountain which was Lady Eleanor Cecily Clifton's memorial to her husband John Talbot Clifton who died in 1882. Lytham Post Office stands next to Speaks draper's shop. Tram tracks were laid down Church Road in 1896.

69 Looking towards St Anne's from the pierhead, *left*, c.1893, showing the sweetshop and narrow 18 ft.-wide deck. By this time William Porritt had built up most of North Promenade. When this photo was taken there was no *Southdown* Hydro (Town Hall), *Majestic Hotel* or Congregational Church.

70 Hydro Terrace, St Anne's Road West, c.1905, *below left*, was erected in St Anne's Square c.1890 as private residences. In the centre was *Miss Tuke's Hydropathic Establishment*. In 1907 these buildings were converted to shops and Miss Tuke opened *The Gables Hydro* at the corner of Orchard and Richmond Roads. The buildings pictured today house Booth's grocers, John Menzies and Winstons.

71 The Double stanner, *below*, looking towards St Anne's c.1893. The Double Stanner was a ridge of shingle which stretched along the beach from St Anne's to Granny's Bay at Ansdell. When Thomas Riley started developing Fairhaven he enclosed the stanner, strengthened it and formed Fairhaven Lake which was filled with water in August 1893.

72 In 1893 Fairhaven, which was on the seaward side of Clifton Drive, between Lytham and St Anne's, consisted of 264 acres of sand-dune. To overcome this, Thomas Riley imported machines known as steam navvies, nicknamed 'American Devils'. These were used to pull down the high sand-dunes and fill the dells, levelling out the estate in readiness for streets and houses.

73 In order to move sand and building materials around Fairhaven Estate a railway was laid down. It came off the main line, running down St Paul's Avenue, encircling the lake and then through the dunes, finishing halfway down Cartmell Road. Two engines, 'Fairhaven' and 'Preston', ran on these tracks; both came from the Hudswell Clarke Railway Foundry. The railway was removed about 1917.

74 St Anne's Road West, viewed from the pier *c*.1894. To the left are houses in St George's Road. In the Square is Hydro Terrace and, opposite, shops are under construction. The building on the right was a school and is now part of the Town Hall. From the pier, St Anne's Road provided an uninterrupted view for over a mile inland.

75 St Anne's Grammar School for Boys, Clifton Drive South, seen here, *above left*, *c*.1894. The headmaster for many years was J.R. Bannister, B.A. and the school course included Latin, French, sciences, singing and drawing. At this time there were 20 private schools in St Anne's and a further 11 at Lytham. This building now houses the offices of the Football League.

76 St Anne's Pier, *left*, in October 1894, after a storm cast adrift a small fishing boat which ploughed through the cast-iron supports bringing a section of the pier deck down and thus marooning the pier-head. In the distance are houses on North Promenade and the Ormerod Home.

77 The Bungalow, *above*, was built for Manchester solicitor Mr. H.T. Crofton in 1894. It stood on a sand-dune (now corner of the Promenade Road and Cartmell Road) on the Fairhaven Estate. The estate railway passed in front, and behind it was a pond known to local schoolboys as 'Froggy Pond'. Later acquired by Mr. A. Rogerson and then Lord Ashton, it was demolished *c*.1960.

78 Seafront villas on South Promenade, St Anne's, 1895. The promenade itself was 'more or less level clay and pebbles' on which the local children played hockey, football and lacrosse. Following the St Anne's Improvement Act (1896), The L & B Co. handed over the promenade to the local council, who added the bandstand and laid out the gardens there.

79 South Promenade, 1995: compare the view below with picture 78. Since 1980 the number of homes for the elderly, such as *The Grove*, has increased dramatically, creating jobs and saving many larger buildings from demolition. Millions of pounds of private capital have been invested in the tourist and leisure industries over the last ten years, transforming hotels and improving facilities for visitors.

80 Canon Hawkins was vicar of St Cuthbert's Parish Church from 1870 to 1914, but lost his sight in 1892. In October 1895 he acquired this tricycle to help him get about. In 1910 he visited a Moslem village in the African desert and wrote home that even the Arab world was more ahead than Lytham in some forms of civilisation.

81 The *Fairhaven Hotel* from Clifton Drive, *c*.1918. Erected in 1895 by Boddington's Brewery on Marine Drive overlooking Granny's Bay and the lake, it was demolished in 1976 and replaced by flats and the present public house. Fairhaven Golf Club was formed in 1895, with links alongside Fairhaven Lake and the Double Stanner. The lake-side café was their original clubhouse.

82 A Blackpool, St Anne's and Lytham tram (1896-1903). These trundled along Clifton Drive belching out gas fumes almost suffocating the passengers. Lop-sided, due to the large encased flywheel, they often came off the track at curves and occasionally, when they reached Squires Gate Bridge, passengers had to get out and push. These were replaced by electric trams in 1903.

83 From the early 1880s Arthur and Rose Holloway managed the *St Anne's Hotel*. Despite her husband's death Rose stayed on there and the hotel flourished, attracting visitors and golfers. She went on to build the *Grand Hotel* (pictured) which opened in 1898. After her death in 1912 her daughter Kitty managed the hotel. In the hotel grounds is the Holloways' pet cemetery.

84 Montauban School for boys, Clifton Drive South, with St Anne's Square to the left, 1896. Established by the Misses Surr in 1875, the school was enlarged in 1894-5 and converted to shops and offices *c.*1920. Today it houses the Sutcliffe family's newsagent. Gill & Reads Ironmongers was erected on the adjoining plot in 1898; occupied by Burton's tailors from 1930, it is now 'Motorworld'.

85 St Anne's Square 1896 looking inland with the junction of Orchard Road to the right. Stead's West End Pharmacy (centre) was erected in 1892 and transformed into the Stancliffe stone-fronted Williams Deacon's Bank in 1912-13; this is now the Royal Bank of Scotland. The shop on the opposite corner is now the National Westminster Bank.

86 The Crescent and corner of Park Road, St Anne's in 1896. To the right is Walmsley & Son, drapers, dressmakers and milliners, which was established in 1883. Since *c.*1970 their shop has been in Wood Street. Other shops include J. Howarth, John Pickup, grocer, the Misses Ingham, toy and fancy goods dealers, as well as James Redfern butchers, established in 1888.

87 St Andrew's Road South from the Crescent in 1896, by which time the Post Office had moved from Alpha House into the next block. In the early years, before this road was so built up, some residents would spend summer days sitting in their front gardens with a gun in their lap taking occasional pot-shots at the rabbits in the dunes opposite.

88 Wood Street, St Anne's, 1896, looking inland from its junction with Orchard Road. At this time there were only three shops in Wood Street and it remained a residential street until after the First World War, when the demand for shops increased. The buildings pictured today house offices of the Inenco Group, Lytham St Anne's Express, St Anne's Carpet Centre and Margaret's Florists Shop.

89 Fairhaven Lake and Golf Links after the sea broke through the sea wall during a storm on 6 October 1896. The photograph was taken from opposite St Paul's Avenue, looking towards Lytham. The golf club's bungalow is in the distance; the railway track to the left is now Inner Promenade. The club subsequently moved; the bungalow later became the Lakeside Café.

90 Clifton Street 1898 looking east, with the new *Ship* and Royal Buildings towering above the old shops and houses. To the right is the garden of Dr. Luke Fisher's house which was pulled down to make way for the new post office and Williams Deacon's Bank in 1899.

91 Clifton Street, looking west towards Clifton Square, 1898. On the left is Richard Maries florist; his nursery was at Mythop and is now Ashton's. Other shops include Mrs. Hayward's Berlin Woolshop and Rowsons Painters and Plumbers. The rest of the shops were demolished to make way for Seymour Mead's establishment.

92 Clifton Square, Lytham, viewed from Henry Street, 1898. The sign to the left reads 'E. Fletcher Practical Confectioner, picnic & garden parties supplied'. When the gas trams reached Lytham the vehicles took in water at the tram depot in Henry Street and whilst the engines cooled the driver and staff had time for a stroll round the shops or a shave at the market.

93 The *Southdown Hydropathic* opened in 1898. In 1925 it was converted for use as the Town Hall. The bandstand was also erected in 1898 and was part of the Improvement Scheme which included shelters and rockeries. John Allen, founder of Kilgrimol School, described these as 'monkey houses and potato hogs' and South Promenade residents protested because the scheme would ruin their sea view. *Left.*

94 St Anne's Public Hall and Assembly Rooms were erected by a private company on the corner of St George's Road and Garden Street in 1901. About 1911 the Assembly Rooms were converted into a picture house, later becoming the *Palace Cinema.* After its closure the ground floor became an indoor market and the upper floor devoted to Fylde Freemasonry. *Below right.*

95 The *County and Commercial Hotel, c.*1905. This was built on the site of the *Market Hotel* and the *Commercial Inn.* In the 1820s there was a palisaded ornamental garden opposite, where the Market Hall now stands. *Below.*

96 *The Victoria Hotel,* Church Road, St Anne's, pictured shortly after its completion, *c.*1898. Early licensees were Edward Howarth and Hugh Ashton. The site of Beauclerk Gardens and the hotel was previously occupied by Whiteside's Farm. In the 1960s a workman digging in the gardens found a 17th-century hoard of coins.

97 The Manchester Home in Clifton Drive North, St Anne's, *c.*1901. This home was built and furnished by Sir William Agnew who on 13 November 1897 declared it open and handed it over to the trustees of the Manchester Children's Hospital for their use as a convalescent home. It stood alongside the Ormerod Home and was demolished in 1972.

47105 St Annes-on-Sea, Manchester Childrens Hospital

98 In 1897 the present links of the Lytham & St Anne's Golf Club were laid out. The old course was required for building purposes. The new clubhouse, seen here from the links *c*.1903, was opened by the Marquis of Lorne (later the Duke of Argyll) on 7 March 1898. The club acquired its 'Royal' prefix in May 1926.

99 The new mock-Tudor entrance to St Anne's Pier, viewed from the deck in 1899. Designed by J.D. Harker, it incorporated tollbooths and offices. Above was the boardroom of the St Anne's Land & Building Company which overlooked their pier and square mile of estate. Since 1953 this side of the building has been obscured by the amusement arcade.

100 St Anne's fire brigade was formed after a blaze in August 1887 reduced a house on South Promenade to a pile of charred timber and four bare walls. Pictured here is the 'Metropolitan' steam fire engine, capable of delivering 260 gallons of water per minute, purchased by St Anne's U.D.C. in November 1900. A fire station was erected in 1902 and replaced in 1985.

101 St Anne's Urban District Council's purpose-built offices on Clifton Drive South were opened on 22 January 1902. This building housed the council and committee rooms, offices for clerk, rate collector, nuisance inspector, surveyor and medical officer of health. In the grounds at the rear were glasshouses where plants were raised for bedding out on the promenade.

102 A now politically incorrect postcard from the turn of the century. 'Niggers' and 'coons', along with minstrels and Pierrots, gave a short performance on Lytham Green in the afternoon to publicise their show in the pier pavilion later that day.

Lytham.

Niggers on Beach.

103 Hastings Place, Lytham, *c.*1902, showing the *County and Commercial Hotel*, Clifton Estate Office and Lytham Conservative Club (opened June 1905). The elm tree was known as 'Old Tom' and, when Lytham Commissioners had the posts and chains put round it, a full set of stocks in excellent preservation were unearthed. 'Old Tom' fell victim to Dutch Elm Disease and was over 240 years old when it was replaced by 'Young Tom' in 1983.

104 A superb photograph of 'The Great Walk' on 1 July 1903 passing over the skew bridge at Ansdell along with a procession of cyclists and motor cars. This was a walking race from Manchester which passed through Lytham on the way to the finishing line at Blackpool. Mr. J. Butler of London (pictured) won the race, covering the 51¼ miles in eight hours, 19 minutes and 50 seconds.

105 Lowther College for Girls, Church Road, Lytham, *c*.1903, opened in the 1890s and was run by Mrs. Florence Lindley. By 1919 there were 160 boarders from all over the country. Extensions had been planned but could not proceed because of the high cost of building just after the war. This school closed in June 1920 and moved to Bodelwyddan Castle near Colwyn Bay.

106 Clifton Drive North, looking towards St Anne's, *c*.1913. To the right are the Manchester and Ormerod Convalescent Homes. To the left are dunes near Highbury Road. These were occupied in the summer months by the Manchester & Salford Wood Street Mission's holiday camp for slum children. Electric trams replaced gas trams in 1903, taking their power from overhead cables.

107 Ansdell Old Station, looking towards Lytham in 1903. Originally a halt and level crossing at Ansdell Road, this station was erected *c.*1878 when the Lytham Land and Building Company started developing land between Cambridge Road and Clifton Drive. The footbridge, which is still standing, was erected in 1901. The present station and railway bridge were opened in 1903. The old station became a goods yard and depot.

108 Pollux Gate, Fairhaven, *c.*1903, looking towards St Anne's. The three ladies are passing the Estate Company's office. The three buildings in the distance stand in Cyprus Avenue, Myra Road and St Paul's Avenue, the latter being the clubhouse of Fairhaven Golf Club (1900-24). The St Anne's end of the estate developed quickly, the Lytham end slowly, and the land in between was leased to Fairhaven Golf Club until 1924.

109 Fairhaven Lake, *c.*1905, where an annual regatta and sports day was held from 1900. Buildings on Inner Promenade and Clifton Drive include the *Fairhaven Hotel*, High Lea, Stanner Bank, Methodist Mission Church and Lytham College for Boys.

110 Clifton Street, *c*.1905, showing the new post office and the new shops occupied by William Cookson and Seymour Mead & Co. The electric tram is on tracks which were extended to Lytham Hospital in 1903.

111 In 1902-4 the Land and Building Company spent over £20,000 improving St Anne's pier. The whole structure was doubled in width and, at the pierhead, shops were erected and an open-air concert enclosure was formed. A magnificent Moorish-style pavilion, capable of seating 920 people, was also added. The 'new pier' opened on 2 April 1904.

The Pier Pavilion, St. Annes-on-the-Sea

Spring Bros., Publishers and Printers, St. Annes-on-the-Sea.

112 Fred Carlton came to this coast in 1894 and his concert party troop known as 'Cousin Freddie's White Coons' was very popular both in Lytham and St Anne's. In 1904 the Fairhaven Estate Company allowed him to use two sites for alfresco entertainment, one on the sands at Granny's Bay and the other in the dunes near St Anne's.

113 Carlton's Cosy Corner, a stage and enclosure in the dunes opposite Riley Avenue, St Anne's. From 1904-34 it drew huge crowds. By 1921 'Wilkie' Warren was entertaining there and, by 1935, when the enclosure was removed to North Beach, 'Freddie Magpie' had charge of it.

114 St Anne's Post Office, Wood Street, *c*.1904. The postmaster, Edwin B. Laycock, is standing in the doorway, and nearby are his children. The door to the right led to a dentist's surgery and the two children used to cup their ears to the wall and listen to the patients' screams. The present post office opened in 1923. The building pictured is now 'Celebrations' Card Shop.

115 St Anne's Square, looking from Clifton Drive on Saturday, 11 June 1904. The procession is part of the annual St Anne's Gala and children's sports day. The first gala was held in 1898 and from 1920 it was known as Hospital Fête Day, raising funds for the War Memorial Hospital. Since about 1949 St Anne's Carnival has been raising money for local charities.

116 St Paul's Church, Clifton Drive, viewed from Lake Road, *c.*1905. This church was erected in 1904 to serve the residents of Ansdell and Fairhaven. Fairhaven, Pollux Gate, Cyprus Avenue and Miletas Place all take their names from St Paul's travels. Holcombe, Lake Road was home to Frederick Holt who, at Christmas 1919, murdered Kathleen Breaks in the sand dunes at St Anne's.

117 The Lytham St Anne's Golf Club moved to its present site in 1897. A second club, the Old Links, was created and from June 1901 played over part of the old course. The event pictured is the opening of the Old Links Clubhouse (now the British Legion Club) in Mayfield Road on 10 June 1905. Their present course opened on 21 January 1911.

118 Jesseta Lees, Lytham Rose Queen, 1905. To her left is the blind Canon Hawkins and, in the light suit, is Edward R. Lightwood, headmaster of Pembroke House School. On the extreme right is Crimean War veteran Augustus Wykeham Clifton of Warton Hall. He was the Squire's great uncle and crowned all the Rose Queens from 1894-1914.

119 Green Drive, *c.*1905, part of the old road from Lytham Hall to Warton via Saltcotes Farm and Lodge Hall. This avenue of trees was given to the town in 1905 but Dutch Elm Disease wrought havoc in the late 1970s and early '80s. It is now a shadow of its former self.

120 *Hugh Gaskell's Commercial Hotel* and training quarters for footballers, 60 Clifton Street, Lytham in 1905, 'shilling dinners served 12-2 and twopenny teas at any hour'. The premises of Thomas Bennett, practical watchmaker, are to the right in the 'Wykeham Cottages'. These were pulled down to erect the Palace Cinema (1930), now the site of Woolworths. The hotel is now a shoe shop.

121 In the 1906 General Election the Blackpool Division was contested by Wilfred Ashley, Conservative, and Vivian Phillips, Liberal. Mr. Ashley is pictured here addressing employees at Lytham Shipyard, unaware that they have scrawled 'Vote for Phillips' on the hustings.

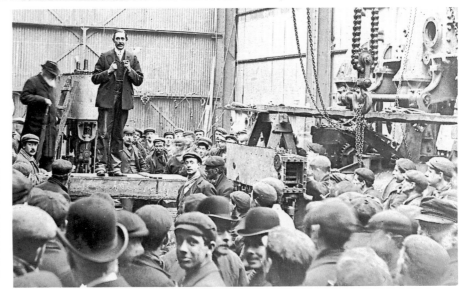

Removal Scenes at the Workhouse.

Friday, June 21st, 1907.

122   The Fylde Board of Guardians was created in 1838. They built a workhouse in the main street at Kirkham to replace a poorhouse in Marsden Street. In 1903-7 they erected a new workhouse at Wesham (now the Park Hospital) at a cost of £50,000. The well-off regarded it as a pauper's paradise and the poor feared it.

123 The Methodist mission in Albert Street, Lytham. Erected in 1907, it was demolished in the 1980s.

124 King Edward VII School for boys, Fairhaven, was erected by the Lytham Charities Trust, set up after the inundation of 1719. It was built at a cost of nearly £60,000, and opened on 22 September 1908 with four masters. The first headmaster was Mr. H. Bompas-Smith.

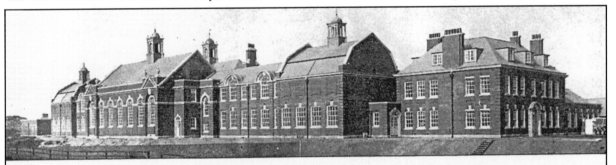

KING EDWARD VII, SCHOOL, LYTHAM.

This handsome educational establishment has been completed to the extent shown in the illustration during the past year. It is situated on the Clifton Drive, the main road between Lytham and St. Annes, and the School is placed on the south easterly portion of the site, at the junction of the inner promenade at Fairhaven and St. Paul's Avenue.

The buildings now erected comprise Assembly Hall, 80ft. by 40ft. wide, Cloak Room, Masters' and Prefects' Rooms, with ten Class rooms of varying sizes. Large Art room and Museum, Physics Laboratory, and two Chemical Laboratories for Senior and Junior Students, with the requisite Preparation rooms, Lecture room, etc. A Master's House is also part of the scheme, with a Dining Hall for the Students and a suite of kitchens attached. The whole is arranged in the form of a hollow square, with inner quadrangle, all the various departments communicating by broad and well-lighted corridors and cloisters. The buildings are mostly two stories in height and are built of red bricks, with white stone dressings, and green slated roofs. The style of the elevations is English Rennaissance, and the grouping presents a commanding and pleasing effect. The architects are Briggs, Wolstenholme and Thornley, Fs.R.I.B.A., of Liverpool and Blackburn, their design being chosen from a number submitted in competition, Professor Beresford Pite being the Assessor.

125 Workmen constructing St Joseph's Roman Catholic Church, Ansdell, *c*.1908. This Gothic-style church was designed by Pugin & Pugin and built in stone at a cost of about £13,000. Bishop Whiteside laid the foundation stone in August 1909 and it was opened by him in September 1914.

126 The Baptist Movement at Ansdell grew rapidly from a bethel opened on 11 November 1903 to a mission church 12 months later. Architects Haywood and Harrison of Accrington designed the present Gothic church and the foundation stones were laid on 11 January 1908. This church, pictured here under construction by Smith Bros. of Burnley and Blackpool, was opened on 17 October 1908.

127 In 1909 and 1910, when most people had never seen an aeroplane, Blackpool held aviation meetings on Layton Hawes (now Blackpool Airport). This photograph shows Grahame-White's biplane which, in August 1910, made a forced landing on the sands opposite North Promenade, St Anne's. His mechanics arrived, breakfasted with him on the beach, fixed the engine fault, and he flew off.

128 St Anne's Council School, in Sydney Street, was opened on 29 August 1910 and for the first 25 years the headmaster was Mr. J.E. Fallowfield. This is now the site of a nursery and day-care centre.

129 The *Imperial Hydropathic*, North Promenade, St Anne's, 1910, surmounted by Hygeia, goddess of health. Opened at Christmas 1910, there were 200 bedrooms after extensions in 1914. A military hospital from 1915-18, it was renamed the *Majestic Hotel* in 1920. Gerald Bright (Geraldo) and his orchestra played there regularly and it housed Civil Service departments 1939-45. Demolished in 1976, it was replaced by flats.

130 The Primitive Methodist Church on the corner of Clifton Drive and King's Road, St Anne's. Officially opened by Sir William Hartley on 7 August 1911, it was distinct from the Wesleyan Methodist churches. It survived the Methodist Union of 1932 but the high cost of repairs resulted in its closure in 1968. A block of flats now stands on the site.

131 Lytham Yacht Club, decorated for the Coronation of George V in 1911. The club's headquarters were in Lytham Baths & Assembly Rooms.

132 In its early days Lytham Pier hosted open-air band performances at the pierhead. By 1893 this area had been enclosed and was later roofed over to form a floral hall and refreshment rooms. Here, concerts were given daily in the season by, amongst others, Miss Dorothea Vincent's Cremona Orchestra, seen here in 1911.

133 In 1909-10 a floral hall was erected on St Anne's Pier. Opened in 1910, it housed the pier orchestra which gave concerts each summer for 57 years. The first conductress was Kate Erl, 1910-20 succeeded by: from 1921-33 Clarice Dunington, 1934-42 William Rees, 1943-64 Lionel Johns and 1965-6 Norman George.

134 The Empire de Luxe Picture Palace was erected in St George's Road, St Anne's and opened on 5 August 1912. Designed by Arnold England, it seated over 900 people. In 1930 the building was enlarged but from the early 1950s audiences began to dwindle. It was later renamed The Plaza and now houses a casino and bingo club.

135 Fairhaven Golf Links, *c.*1914. The photographer is standing near what is today The Boulevard, looking towards Lytham. In the distance is the side of King Edward VII School and to its left the clubhouse (1900-24) in St Paul's Avenue. Builders encroached on this land and the club moved to its present site in Lytham Hall Park in 1924.

136 A postcard showing Bolton Wanderers 'in training' outside the *Ship & Royal Hotel*, Lytham, *c.*1914. Before the First World War, Lytham and Fairhaven were popular training grounds for Lancashire football teams.

137 The Blackburn Convalescent Home was built by the Blackburn Charity Organisation Society at a cost of £12,000 and opened in 1915 amongst the sand dunes off North Drive. In October 1924 extensions costing £7,000 were opened, increasing the accommodation to about sixty. This building is now semi-derelict.

138 Soldiers of the Royal Field Artillery, *above*, in the fields by Headroomgate Road, St Anne's, where they had riding schools. Houses in the distance are on Highbury Road. These brigades trained in Lytham and St Anne's between February and August 1915; this photograph was taken on 14 June during 'the particularly hot summer which resulted in a drought and faces as brown as berries'.

139 Lord Derby inspecting the 151st and 148th R.F.A. brigades on Lytham Green, 16 April 1915, *left*. Lytham and St Anne's were used for the initial training of 4,000 soldiers. At first many drilled in civilian clothes using wooden guns. Later, uniforms and guns arrived, as did horses from South America, some of which had never been shod. Four brigades trained in Lytham Hall Park.

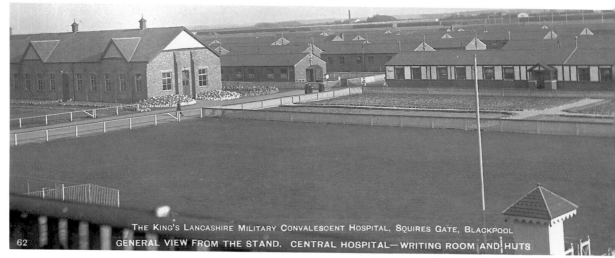

THE KING'S LANCASHIRE MILITARY CONVALESCENT HOSPITAL, SQUIRES GATE, BLACKPOOL

62 GENERAL VIEW FROM THE STAND. CENTRAL HOSPITAL—WRITING ROOM AND HUTS

140 The King's Lancashire Military Convalescent Hospital at Squire's Gate (Blackpool Airport site), *above*, was opened in September 1915 with accommodation for 2,000 wounded soldiers. Here, the soldiers recuperated, were given additional training and were sent back to the front. This view shows the long lines of huts that housed the soldiers; the destructor chimney off Kilnhouse Lane, St Anne's, is in the distance.

141 After the last R.F.A. brigades left the area in August 1915, Lytham was used to billet and train soldiers from the Pioneer Battalions. They are seen here, *below*, on Lytham Green during a sports day; in the distance is Lytham Windmill (burned out on 1 January 1919) and the Custom House. St Anne's was used to accommodate convalescent soldiers and officers.

142 In 1913 St Anne's U.D.C. proposed to purchase St George's Gardens. Many ratepayers protested and the scheme was put to the vote. On the eve of the poll, Lord Ashton of Lancaster intervened with a gift of £21,350 and further sums to purchase the gardens and additional land for the town. 'Ashton Gardens' and the new Ashton pavilion were opened in 1916.

143 St Anne's Council spent £18,000 erecting open-air swimming baths on the beach. Opened by Wilfred Ashley M.P. on 10 June 1916, sun-bathing facilities were added in 1930, Art Deco café in 1937, and a heating system in 1972. Several cold seasons, low attendances and prohibitive repair costs resulted in their closure in 1988. A private company built 'Pleasure Island' on this site in 1991.

144 St Anne's Railway Station staff and mascot during the First World War. A roll of honour lists company employees away on active service; women conductors have been introduced to fill their places. The tram company employed women conductors from June 1915 and women drivers from May 1916. Classes at St Anne's Technical School trained girls in skills required to enter the workplace.

145 St Anne's Pier, *c.*1919, and the *Imperial Hydro* (renamed the *Majestic Hotel* in 1920). The year 1919 was an exceptional one for holiday resorts nationally. War workers and others had been cooped up in offices and workshops for four long years; tens of thousands of soldiers had been demobbed. This first holiday season after the Armistice lasted from Easter to October.

146 Thomas Bannister erected 'Banastre Holme', *above*, on St Anne's Road East in 1897 at a cost of £20,000. In 1920 it was purchased for £10,000 and converted into St Anne's War Memorial Hospital. This was opened by Lord Derby on Charter Day, 1 May 1922, when Lytham and St Anne's were united as a Borough. Operated by the N.H.S. since about 1949, it has now closed.

147 Pot Stall, St Anne's Market, St David's Road South, *c.1922, above right*. The market was designed by Arnold England and erected by Keenan Parker & Yates with a 'handsome front elevation in terracotta'. It was fronted by 16 lock-up shops and five rows of stalls, 60 of which were occupied by August 1922. Later a co-operative store, it is now the Kwik Save supermarket.

148 Blackpool Road, Ansdell, *right*. The municipal bus service began on 4 August 1923 and was described as a great boon to people who lived a 'long way from nowhere', i.e. away from the tram route. Two buses started running every half-hour between St Anne's and Lytham. The cost of a full journey was fourpence. Buses replaced trams altogether in 1937.

149 The unveiling of St Anne's War Memorial, Sunday, 12 October 1924, witnessed by a crowd of 15,000 people. Designed by Sir Walter Marsden, M.C., it cost £10,000 to erect and was the gift of Lord Ashton. A bronze tablet recorded the names of 170 men who fell in the First World War. Lytham cenotaph contains 192 names and was unveiled in January 1922.

150 St Anne's Railway Station, rebuilt in 1925, viewed from the Crescent, *c*.1932. The 'Club train' stopped here each morning. In this exclusive 'Club' there were 60 members—merchants and businessmen—who commuted between the coast and Manchester in special 'sumptuously appointed carriages'. Soft drinks were served by an attendant.

151 Clifton Drive North, 29 October 1927, looking towards St Anne's from the Ormerod Home. The previous night's gales drove a high tide over the dunes flooding North Drive to a depth of six feet. The flagstaff at Royal Lytham was 'broken in two like a twig'. At Lytham a dyke burst, flooding houses in Preston Road. Similar floods occurred in 1977.

DINING HALL.

LOUNGE

CORNER OF ONE OF THE BEDROOMS

WRITING & READING ROOM.

SOUVENIR
OF
WEST YORKS MINERS'
CONVALESCENT HOME
"WESTWOOD"   LYTHAM.
E.2747.

152 'Westwood', *left*, a large Victorian house overlooking Lytham Cricket Club, was home to the Cliftons' agent, Thomas Fair, in the 1890s. In 1928 it was converted into the West Yorkshire Miners' Home. This building was demolished *c.*1982 to make way for Westwood Mews.

153 The old baths at Lytham, *below*, were rebuilt in 1927-8 by Lytham St Anne's Corporation. They were given a palatial new frontage to Dicconson Terrace and opened in June 1928. This frontage was retained when the rest of the baths were demolished in 1990. The building now contains flats, new assembly rooms, offices and Lytham Yacht Club.

154 St Anne's Cricket Club, *above*, was formed in 1879. Before the First World War its pitch was in fields off St David's Road North. War stopped play but the club was revived in 1924 and acquired its new pitch at Highbury Road, seen here in 1928 with the tea and cricket pavilions. There were also three grass and two hard tennis courts.

155 Lytham Palace Cinema *c*.1935, erected by the Blackpool Tower Co. from designs by Mr. F.G.M. Chancellor. It had a cream-coloured faience front and, above, a panelled frieze, in cream with a blue background. An Egyptian theme was carried on throughout with painted panels and friezes. It opened on Easter Monday 1930 on a site now occupied by Woolworths.

156 Queen Mary School, Fairhaven, 1943, with new houses to the right and air-raid shelters to the left. All this land was part of the Fairhaven Golf Links until 1924. Built at a cost of over £80,000, this school opened on 23 September 1930 with 153 girls. The first headmistress was Miss Doris Bailey, M.Sc.

157 Lytham St Anne's Chamber of Trade promoted the Borough in 1930-1 by running this illuminated tramcar through to Blackpool. During the years of the Depression local shops suffered because many residents were traders, agents and manufacturers in the depressed industrial cities. Other residents relied on their incomes from share dividends. Some residents lost everything, others had to live in reduced circumstances.

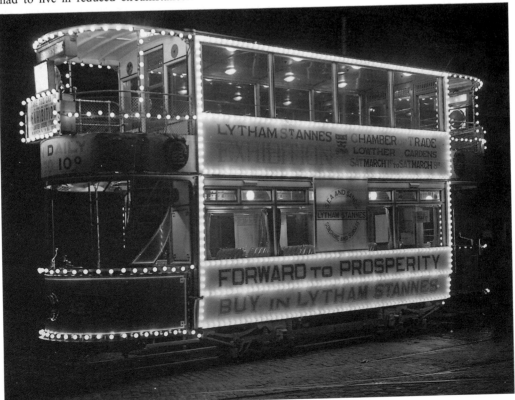

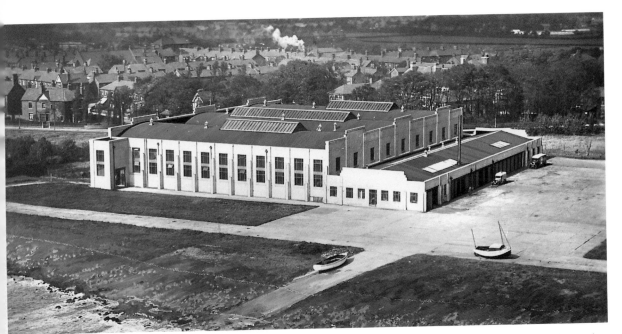

158 In the 1930s the Corporation constructed this paddling pool on Lytham beach, *above left*. Beyond the pier purification tanks were built so that mussels from the sewage-polluted Ribble could be made fit for human consumption. This provided employment for local men. Lytham pier, which had lost its pavilion in the fire of 1928, was closed in 1938 and demolished in 1960.

159 Cookson's Exhibition Bakery, East Beach, Lytham, *above*. These buildings were constructed for use as a flying boat factory in 1918. The aeroplanes were taken down the ramp and launched on the shore. This closed in the 1920s and the Parkstone Film Company purchased them. In 1938 Cookson's, which was already established in Lytham, had the buildings reconstructed as their exhibition bakery.

160 During 1934-9 the Corporation built the Outer Promenade at St Anne's, *left*. This enclosed the existing baths and the new miniature golf course and boating pool. An enterprising scheme, it provided much-needed employment. It was economical because shingle taken from the beach was converted to aggregate in a stone crusher and used in construction. Aggregate was also sold to local builders.

161 St Anne's Square, looking towards the pier *c*.1935. The Square was not 'completed' until 1925 when Heap's erected St Anne's Buildings (since 1957, Woolworths). In 1930 Burton's opened their tailor's shop in Gill & Read's old premises (now Motorworld) and in 1931 the road was widened. One of the most spacious shopping centres in England, there was a host of interesting, high-class shops.

G.3632.

162 *The Southdown Hydro* was converted into the town hall for the new Borough of Lytham St Anne's in 1924-5. This photograph shows men delivering two figures there *c.*1935; these have since graced the entrance. In the 1930s Ald Dawson and others donated many works of art to the Borough; it was intended to build a municipal art gallery but this never materialised.

163 King George VI and Queen Elizabeth on the dais erected at the pier entrance, St Anne's, during the royal visit of 1938. Back in 1913 King George V and Queen Mary passed through Lytham and St Anne's during a motoring tour of Lancashire and in 1928 Prince Edward visited Lytham.

164 An unusual postcard view of Fascist graffiti, August Bank Holiday, 1939. Lytham St Anne's was not considered to be a hotbed of malcontent Fascists and so it came as a shock to many when this slogan appeared overnight, tarred onto the sea-facing wall of St Anne's open-air baths. This was the eve of the Second World War.

165 William Rees conducting the orchestra in the Floral Hall, St Anne's Pier, Easter 1940, *left*. The orchestra played each summer season throughout the war; Lionel Johns became conductor in 1943. Hay & Lane's Summer Revellers, 1940, was the last summer show in the Moorish Pavilion until Edward Kent's Starlight Gaieties in 1952.

166 House in Church Road, St Anne's, *below left*, after a German raid, 1 October 1940. When in 1939 Government inspectors came to examine wartime emergency provisions, the question of mortuary accommodation was raised. Their reply was, 'Oh you mustn't bother about a mortuary. The public must get used to seeing the bodies laid out in rows in the open'. Fortunately, casualties were light.

167 Blackpool Sea Cadets, *below*, parading through St Anne's Square during 'Warship Week', March 1942, when Lytham St Anne's adopted a warship named *The Queenborough*. Shops include: Sandbach's Café and Confectioners; Thomas Talbot, fruiterer; John Chadwick, tobacconist and ladies hairdresser; Rosenberg, draper and Salida's Gown Shop.

168 The architect's plan of proposed War Memorial Homes, Lytham St Anne's, 1949. These were erected as a memorial to local men killed in the Second World War. Situated at the corner of Church Road and Smithy Lane, the scheme included a small chapel.

169 The housing shortage after the Second World War led to the erection of many prefabricated homes throughout Lytham St Anne's. More permanent homes were built later, the largest scheme being a council estate in the fields off Kilnhouse Lane, St Anne's, pictured here in 1953. An industrial estate was subsequently established alongside, creating many jobs.

170 Sand Yacht, St Anne's, 1955. In the early 1950s four local men obtained permission from the Corporation to run their home-made sand yacht on the beach at St Anne's. The sport became popular and the Fylde Sand Yacht Club was formed. This club held the first international meeting with Belgians, French and Germans participating. Regular meetings are held on North Beach, St Anne's.

171 The *Links Hotel* was erected in Heeley Road, St Anne's in 1955-6 to serve the growing community in that area. This photograph shows the interior of this new public house. Other new post-war public houses were the *Queensway*, *The Blossoms*, the *Hole in One*, *The Bounty* and *Porters*.

172 One of the few post-war Corporation schemes to enhance attractions in the Borough was the miniature railway on South Promenade, St Anne's, completed in 1956.

173 The picturesque Gillett's Cross Slack Farm, off Highbury Road, St Anne's, demolished in 1964. Since the last war the vast majority of the Borough's older dwellings, cottages, farms and lodges once inhabited by tenants of the Clifton Estate, have been demolished. As recently as 1990 Kilnhouse Lane Farm was demolished. So few have survived to remind us of our past that a concerted attempt at preservation is required.

174 Aerial view of Lytham Hall Park, looking south from Ansdell, *c.*1960. Lytham's post-war prosperity was partly due to the Warton aircraft factory and the Land Registry Offices. The Clifton family's long association with Lytham was severed in 1964 when Lytham Hall and Park were sold to G.R.E. The company built offices at Lytham and developed the Hall Park Estate.

175 Aerial view of St Anne's, looking north towards Blackpool, *c.*1970. The war left a legacy of Civil Service departments and the Premium Bonds Office was established here in 1957, though many of these have since moved. The hotel and catering industry has survived by changing to meet modern needs. Since the 1980s nursing and rest homes have flourished, providing many jobs.

176 The entrance to Ansdell & Fairhaven Railway Station, erected on the new Woodlands Road Bridge in 1903, seen here *c.*1970 and demolished, along with platform buildings, in 1972. The extensive station buildings at St Anne's were demolished in 1985 and replaced by a small booking office. Lytham Station is now a public house. The line is now a single track railway.

177 The St Anne's Land & Building Company celebrated its centenary in 1974 culminating on 7 June with a concert given by Yehudi Menuhin in the Moorish Pavilion attended by Princess Anne. Six weeks later, on 20 July, fire engulfed the pavilion. The raging inferno (seen here from the *Majestic Hotel*) reduced the Edwardian Moorish Pavilion to a mass of tangled metal and charred wood.

178 Clifton Street, Lytham, 1995; compare this with illustration 91. Large numbers of office-workers both live and work near the centre of Lytham. Their patronage of shops there has helped to retain much of its unique character and charm.

179 St Anne's Square, looking from the Crescent, Carnival Day 1992. The graceful Crescent Bridge was designed to sweep gently down, opening out to the spacious St Anne's Square. Unfortunately, The Square is open and exposed to the elements, especially strong winds from the sea. Shelter, pedestrianisation, gardens and a nearby free car-park could help revitalise this centre. It has great potential.

180 East Beach, Lytham, 1991. Compare this with the frontispiece. From the early 1900s the Ribble Navigation Company's 'new channel' resulted in silt and mud being deposited on Lytham Beach. By the 1930s spartina grass had established itself there. It has since spread along the coast to Fairhaven, threatening the beach at St Anne's.

Bibliography

Ashton, W., *Evolution of a Coastline* (1920)

Aspin, C., *Dizzy Heights, The Story of Lancashire's First Flyingmen* (1988)

Brown, K., *Lytham and St Anne's, the Reluctant Resorts* (1990)

Dakres, J.M., *A History of Shipbuilding at Lytham* (1992)

Fishwick, H., *History of Lytham* (1907)

Forshaw, D., *On Those Infernal Ribble Banks* (1992)

Greaves, D.W., *Chats Concerning Heyhouses, Lytham & St Anne's-on-the-Sea Since the Days of 1870 A.D.* (1925)

Harrison, G., *Rage of Sand* (1972)

Kennedy, J. *The Clifton Chronicle* (1990)

Latham, C., *Description of Lytham* (1813)

Lytham Times (1891-99)

Porter, J., *History of the Fylde of Lancashire* (1876)

Preston Pilot (1880-89)

St Anne's-on-the-Sea Express (1898-1920)

Whittle, P., *Marina* (1831)

Wright, G.L., *History of the Lytham Charities* (1950)

Index

THE ESTATE

belonging to

THE St. ANNES-ON-THE-SEA LAND AND BUILDING COMPANY, LIMITED.

ST. PATRICK'S ROAD NORTH

ST. DAVID'S ROAD NORT

Gas Works

From Blackpool

Steam Laundry

LANCASHIRE AND YORKSHIRE AND LONDON AND

Goods Yard

ST. ANDREW'S ROAD NOR

St. George's Gardens

From Blackpool

Convalescent Home

CLIFTON DRIVE NORTH

BEACH ROAD

NORTH PROMENADE

High Water

NOTE,- Plots coloured Pink are Leased.

Scale of Feet.

100 0 100 200 300 400 500   1000   2000

Charles Fox, Lith. 14, Brown St. Manchester.